ellow-Eared Conure	**31** White Rhinoceros	**41** Mandarin Duck	**51** Kakapo
Voolly Spider Monkey	**32** Jackass Penguin	**42** Père David's Deer	**52** Numbat
idigo Macaw	**33** Cape Vulture	**43** Snow Leopard	**53** Takahe
olden Lion Marmoset	**34** African Elephant	**44** Orang-utan	**54** Tuatara
Iorthern Bald Ibis	**35** Mountain Gorilla	**45** Lion-Tailed Macaque	**55** Bowhead Whale
eopard	**36** Indris	**46** Kouprey	**56** Hooded Seal
Valia Ibex	**37** Giant Panda	**47** Philippine Eagle	**57** Mediterranean Monk Seal
irevy's Zebra	**38** Siberian Tiger	**48** Komodo Dragon	**58** Blue Whale
Vhite-Tailed Fish-Eagle	**39** Wild Camel	**49** Leadbeater's Possum	**59** Narwhal
rabian Oryx	**40** Giant Salamander	**50** Bridled Nail-Tailed Wallaby	**60** Loggerhead Turtle

"Some animals he deliberately destroys...other animals find his presence uncongenial and gradually dwindle in numbers or disappear."

James Ritchie
Scottish naturalist, writing in 1920

Foreword
by **Cyril Littlewood** MBE
Founder and Director of the
Young People's Trust for the Environment and Nature Conservation

Earth is a small and fragile planet and we are at last beginning to realize just how fragile it is. Our human population is increasing by more than 90 million each year and we are taking over more and more of the land surface – leaving less for wildlife and wild plants.

Across the world the once teeming populations of wild animal species have been drastically reduced, many to the point of extinction. We are polluting the air we breathe, the land we grow our food on, the water we drink and even the very oceans themselves! This is a pretty gloomy picture on the whole – and yet there is a ray of light and hope shining through. It is created by the way in which today's young people are taking an ever greater interest in conservation and the protection of the environment.

This book will help those young people to realize the plight of just some of today's threatened species. The awful possibility is that children who come across this book in future years may find that some of today's threatened species have become extinct – gone for ever.

Despite this grim possibility, I am of the opinion that today's young people, when they become 'the public' of tomorrow, will want to take much better care of our planet Earth – and I have great faith in their potential ability to do just that!

The Young People's Trust for the Environment and Nature Conservation is dedicated to the education of young people in matters relating to the conservation of the world's natural resources and wild places. It operates a school lecture service, residential 'environmental discovery' courses and a free information service for young people and their teachers (stamped addressed envelope required for reply).
Y.P.T.E.N.C.,
95 Woodbridge Road,
Guildford, Surrey, England GU1 4PY

YPTENC

CHILDREN'S ATLAS OF ENDANGERED ANIMALS

John Malam

animal illustrations by Graham Austin
maps by Phil Harding
designed by Hilary Edwards-Malam

Foreword by Cyril Littlewood MBE

Contents

Introduction to endangered animals

No one alive today has ever seen a living **Dodo**, a **Great Auk** or a **Quagga**. These are just three of the world's many animals which are now extinct. They are gone for good because extinction means for ever.

The **Dodo** was killed for food and its eggs were taken by animals, such as monkeys, which man introduced to its island home. The last time anyone claims to have seen a living Dodo was in 1681. A few years later this species of flightless bird died out. It had been hunted to death. All that remains today is one dried head and a foot, preserved separately in two museums in England.

One day in June 1844, a party of sailors went to Eldey, an island off the coast of Iceland. They went ashore to look for the **Great Auk** – one of the largest sea-birds in the North Atlantic. A collector had paid them to hunt for the Great Auk and its eggs, and on Eldey the sailors discovered a pair of these birds. Both were clubbed to death. There is a story that the female had been sitting on an egg and that it was crushed by one of the sailors as he raced after the helpless pair. Now all that remains are about 80 stuffed birds and 75 eggs, in various collections.

The **Quagga** was a kind of zebra which lived in South Africa. It roamed the plains in large herds and settlers hunted it for its meat and skin. The last wild Quagga was killed in 1878 and the last one of all died in Amsterdam Zoo in 1883. Of the thousands that were once alive, only about 20 stuffed examples and a few photographs now remain.

Great Auk – extinct by 1844

Dodo – extinct by 1681

Scientists have listed about 4,500 animals which are endangered, of which 550 are mammals and 1,000 are birds – the rest are reptiles, amphibians, fishes and insects. Already, man has been involved in the extinction of at least 500 different kinds of animals.

The animals described in this book come from all over the world, and the dangers they face vary from hunting and loss of habitat to such things as tourism and even low-flying aeroplanes.

How rare are they?

Each of the animals described in this book has been given a 'star' to show how much danger it is in.

*	slightly in danger
**	becoming an endangered animal
***	definitely endangered
****	in danger of becoming extinct
*****	virtually extinct

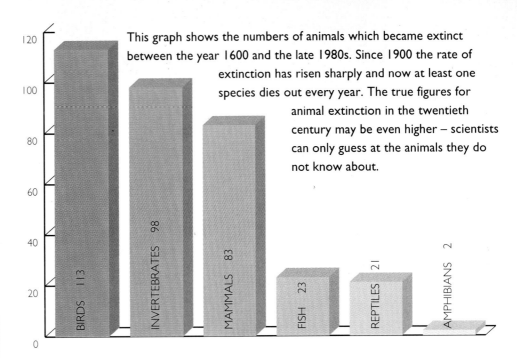

This graph shows the numbers of animals which became extinct between the year 1600 and the late 1980s. Since 1900 the rate of extinction has risen sharply and now at least one species dies out every year. The true figures for animal extinction in the twentieth century may be even higher – scientists can only guess at the animals they do not know about.

BIRDS 113 · INVERTEBRATES 98 · MAMMALS 83 · FISH 23 · REPTILES 21 · AMPHIBIANS 2

Ten animals which have become extinct since 1600

	Common name	Where last seen in the wild	When last seen alive
Mammals	Aurochs (wild cattle)	Poland	1627
	Bluebuck (antelope)	South Africa	1799
	Quagga (zebra)	South Africa	1883
	Steller's Sea Cow (sea lion)	Arctic, Bering Sea	1768
	Tarpan (wild horse)	USSR	1879
Birds	Dodo	Mauritius	1681
	Dusky Sparrow	USA	1988
	Great Auk	Iceland	1844
	Laughing Owl	New Zealand	1915
	Passenger Pigeon	USA	1914

Quagga – extinct by 1883

North and Central Europe and Scandinavia

Austria, Belgium, British Isles, Bulgaria, Czechoslovakia, Denmark, Federal Republic of Germany, Finland, France (north of the Alps), Hungary, Iceland, Luxembourg, The Netherlands, Norway, Poland, Republic of Ireland, Romania, Sweden, Switzerland, Union of Soviet Socialist Republics (USSR: west of the Urals)

❶ As old buildings are destroyed in the British Isles, life for the **Greater Horseshoe Bat** has become difficult. With fewer and fewer places to live it is now an endangered mammal. Another danger comes from the poisonous chemicals which are sprayed on to cereal crops. These are meant to kill harmful insects, but the result is that the Greater Horseshoe Bat finds less insects to eat. Those that it does find may be contaminated with poison – which it eats.

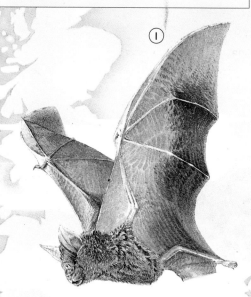

❸ The **Wild Forest Reindeer** has been hunted nearly to extinction. For centuries, hunters have killed it for its antlers and its meat. Its great herds used to contain thousands of animals, but now there are only a few hundred left alive. The last of the Wild Forest Reindeer are to be found in Finland, living in the cold and icy tundra landscape of the Arctic Circle.

❷ Once the **Peregrine Falcon** was a common sight over the British Isles and Northern Europe. Since farmers began to use pesticides on crops, to protect them from harmful creatures, this bird of prey has fallen victim to the poisons. Small animals, such as mice, feed off the poisoned crops and in turn the Peregrine Falcon eats the mice – so the poisons enter its body. Some birds die quickly while others become infertile, which means they cannot raise any young. Also, the eggs of the Peregrine Falcon are sometimes taken by egg thieves – usually humans, not wild animals.

5 The **Flying Squirrel** is a mystery – no one really knows how much danger it is in. It lives in Finland and some parts of Northern Europe. As the trees of its forest home are felled it is being forced to retreat to more isolated areas. In these new areas, the conditions for its survival may not be as good. In recent years the Flying Squirrel has not been seen as often as it used to be, which is why people think it is slowly dying out. The Flying Squirrel does not really fly – it has flaps of skin joining its arms and legs and it glides from tree to tree.

6 Fishermen in Bulgaria and parts of Germany and Romania used to think the **Dalmatian Pelican** was taking all their fish – so they hunted it and set fire to its breeding sites. But it has suffered for another reason. As more land is needed for farming and building, the wetlands where it lives have been drained. Even though the Dalmatian Pelican is now protected by law, some fishermen still kill it because they say it is a nuisance.

4 The **European Bison** has suffered an even worse fate. The forests of Central Europe where it lived were cut down and the last animal living in the wild was killed in the 1920s. Fortunately some had been taken to zoos and the species was kept alive in captivity. In the 1950s some were put back into the wild, from ones bred in zoos. There are now a few European Bison living in the forests of Poland and Romania again. Today it is a protected animal and it cannot be hunted any more. It is also called the Wisent.

Common name	1 Greater Horseshoe Bat	2 Peregrine Falcon	3 Wild Forest Reindeer	4 European Bison	5 Flying Squirrel	6 Dalmatian Pelican
Scientific name	*Rhinolophus ferrumequinum*	*Falco peregrinus*	*Rangifer tarandus fennicus*	*Bison bonasus*	*Pteromys volans*	*Pelecanus crispus*
Where found	British Isles	British Isles, France	Finland	Poland, Romania	Finland	Bulgaria, Germany, Romania, USSR
Main dangers	Pesticides, loss of habitat	Pesticides, egg thieves	Hunting	Hunting, forest clearance	Forest clearance	Hunting, pollution, drainage
How rare?	***	**	***	****	*	****

South Europe

Albania, France (south of the Alps), Greece, Italy, Portugal, Spain, Turkey (part), Yugoslavia

7 The **Spanish Lynx** was once widespread throughout the mountains of Spain and Portugal. Its numbers fell sharply in the 1950s and '60s when a disease called myxomatosis wiped out much of the rabbit population – the main food of the Spanish Lynx. Hunters have also claimed the lives of many of these small cats, trapping them for their fur.

8 Along the banks of fast-flowing mountain streams in Spain and Portugal lives the **Pyrenean Desman**, a small mole-like animal. Water pollution is the main threat to its survival. Water contaminated by harmful chemicals poisons the insects which the Pyrenean Desman eats, and it dies. Also, as mountain streams are blocked or diverted, the Pyrenean Desman is losing its natural home. Unfortunately, this tiny mammal is also caught by hunters who value it for its fur.

9 Another endangered bird in Southern Europe is **Audouin's Gull** which nests in the area of the Tyrrhenian Sea, which is to the west of Italy. It might look like an ordinary gull, but the black stripe on its bill distinguishes it from all others. Fishermen have attacked Audouin's Gull, stealing its eggs and fledglings for food. Tourists have invaded its nesting grounds and forced it to leave for less suitable areas.

Common name	7 Spanish Lynx	8 Pyrenean Desman	9 Audouin's Gull	10 Chamois	11 Hermann's Tortoise	12 Imperial Eagle
Scientific name	*Felis lynx pardina*	*Galemys pyrenaicus*	*Larus audoinii*	*Rupicapra rupicapra*	*Testudo hermanni*	*Aquila heliaca*
Where found	Spain	France, Portugal, Spain	Corsica, Italy, Sardinia	Italy	Greece, Mediterranean coast	Greece, Portugal, Spain, Turkey, Yugoslavia
Main dangers	Hunting, loss of habitat and food supply	Water pollution, hunting, loss of habitat	Egg thieves	Hunting, tourism, persecution	Collecting, land clearance	Hunting, pollution, poisoning, loss of habitat
How rare?	****	***	***	*	***	****

10 The **Chamois** used to inhabit the rocky uplands of north Italy and the Alps in large numbers. But since these areas have become popular for skiing and winter sports, the timid Chamois has been forced into other habitats. It is a protected animal but even so its skin is prized as 'shammy leather' and tufts of its hair are used as decorations in Alpine hats. It is also hunted for meat and for 'trophies' which are used as decorations.

12 One of the rarest birds of prey in Southern Europe is the **Imperial Eagle**. Unlike other eagles, it does not live high up in the mountains. Instead, it prefers open grassland or woods where it hunts for rabbits and other small animals. Because it lives in lowland areas it comes into conflict with man. The Imperial Eagle is in danger from loss of habitat as the countryside where it lives is built over, from poisons in the food it catches and from hunting. It is protected by law – but this is not enough to stop accidents from happening. Overhead wires are a modern danger to the Imperial Eagle and some have died after flying into them.

11 Not very many years ago tortoises were commonly kept as pets. They were gathered in their thousands and exported all over the world. **Hermann's Tortoise** was collected throughout Greece and around the Mediterranean coast and now only a few are left in the wild. Land clearance for new buildings has added to the plight of Hermann's Tortoise, an animal of Southern Europe which has suffered more than most at the hands of man.

North and Central America

Bahamas, Belize, Canada, Costa Rica, Cuba, Dominica, El Salvador, Greenland, Guatemala, Haiti, Honduras, Jamaica, Mexico, Nicaragua, Panama, Puerto Rico, USA

13 The **North American Otter** has been caught by hunters for so long that it is now a very rare sight. Once it was common throughout North America, from the cold rivers in Alaska and Canada to the warmer areas further south in the United States. But its thick fur attracted hunters and they began to kill the North American Otter in their thousands. Today, the main danger is from the polluted water in which the otter swims.

(13)

15 Other names for the **Mountain Lion** are Puma and Cougar. It was once widespread throughout North America, but hunting has taken its toll. Today, only small, isolated populations survive in parts of Canada and the United States. The Mountain Lion eats a wide range of animals, ranging from hares and rabbits to farmers' cattle. It is because it will attack livestock that it has been killed by man.

(14)

14 Amongst the rarest birds in the world is the **California Condor**. It used to live in the mountains of the western United States and despite all the efforts to save this large bird of prey it has died out in the wild. Its decline began in the last century when gold diggers shot the California Condor because they wanted to collect its long, black feathers. In this century, its natural habitat has been invaded by tourists, its food has become poisoned with pesticides and low-flying aeroplanes have disturbed its nesting sites. The only ones alive are kept in zoos – too rare to be put back into the wild.

(15)

16 The national emblem of the United States is the **Bald Eagle** – the rarest eagle in North America. Today it lives mainly in Alaska, hunting for fish in rivers and lakes. One of its favourite fish is salmon and until the 1950s a reward was paid for each Bald Eagle shot. This was to prevent it from taking too many salmon. The Bald Eagle is protected by law today, but now, unfortunately, chemicals used by farmers have entered its food chain. The poisons have caused the females to become infertile or to lay eggs with shells so thin that they break easily.

17 The **Grizzly Bear** (also called the Brown Bear) is the largest meat-eating animal in the world today. But throughout the forests and tundra of North America it has been hunted by man. Sometimes it has been killed because it has attacked farmers' cattle while other times it has been hunted for 'sport'. Wherever possible in North America, the Grizzly Bear is protected by law – but it is still an endangered animal.

18 In the grasslands of the United States, close to the border with Canada, lives North America's rarest mammal. The **Black-Footed Ferret** is so rare that it is on the brink of extinction. As the grasslands are turned into land for farming, the threat to the Black-Footed Ferret comes from poisoning. Farmers put poison down the burrows of animals which eat their crops. Because it also lives in a burrow, it is in danger of being poisoned by accident. As it is so rare, rewards have been offered for sighting a living Black-Footed Ferret. To prove one has been seen a photograph must be taken.

Common name	13 North American Otter	14 California Condor	15 Mountain Lion	16 Bald Eagle	17 Grizzly Bear	18 Black-Footed Ferret
Scientific name	*Lutra canadensis*	*Gymnogyps californianus*	*Felis concolor*	*Haliaeetus leucocephalus*	*Ursus arctos*	*Mustela nigripes*
Where found	Arctic, Canada, United States	United States	Canada, United States	United States	Arctic, Canada, United States, Mexico	United States
Main dangers	Hunting, loss of habitat, water pollution	Hunting, poisoning, tourism, aeroplanes	Hunting	Poisoning, hunting	Hunting, persecution	Poisoning, spread of agriculture
How rare?	***	*****	***	****	***	*****

South America

Argentina, Bolivia, Brazil, Chile, Colombia, Ecuador, French Guiana, Guyana, Paraguay, Peru, Surinam, Uruguay, Venezuela

19 In the forest-covered mountains of South America lives the **Spectacled Bear**. Until quite recently it was safe from harm, but as its forest home has been cut down its numbers have started to fall. Farmers have moved higher into the mountains, clearing the tropical forests as they go. The Spectacled Bear is a protected animal in many parts of South America, but it is still hunted for its thick fur, its meat and its fat.

20 An animal which is not in as much danger is the **Giant Armadillo**, found in many parts of South America. However, the situation could change for the worse because it is vulnerable to the loss of its grass and forest home, turned into pastures for sheep and fields for crops. Also, the Giant Armadillo is the victim of persecution and hunting – its meat is prized by some native South Americans.

21 The **Yellow-Eared Conure** is a parrot from the forests of Colombia and Ecuador. It was once quite a common sight, but the destruction of its forest home has caused its downfall. Now the Yellow-Eared Conure occurs only in very small numbers in remote areas and it is very rarely seen. The places where it lives have been declared national parks in an attempt to save it from dying out for ever.

22 Like others in its family, the **Woolly Spider Monkey** is much sought after by animal collectors, despite this trade being against the law in many countries. It lives in the tropical rainforests of Brazil, but here the constant threat is from habitat destruction. As the great forests are cut down to make way for agriculture, roads and towns, the Woolly Spider Monkey is forced deeper into the interior of the country. It is also prey to the hunter who values it for its meat.

Common name	19 Spectacled Bear	20 Giant Armadillo	21 Yellow-Eared Conure	22 Woolly Spider Monkey	23 Indigo Macaw	24 Golden Lion Marmoset
Scientific name	*Tremarctos ornatus*	*Priodontes maximus*	*Ognorhynchus icterotis*	*Brachyteles arachnoides*	*Anodorhynchus leari*	*Leontopithecus rosalia*
Where found	Bolivia, Ecuador, Peru	Argentina, Brazil, Colombia, Peru, Venezuela	Colombia, Ecuador	Brazil	Brazil	Brazil
Main dangers	Hunting, forest clearance	Loss of habitat, hunting, persecution	Forest clearance	Forest clearance, hunting, illegal trading	Egg thieves, collectors	Forest clearance, illegal trading
How rare?	***	**	**	***	*****	*****

23 Of the many endangered birds in South America, the **Indigo Macaw** (also called Lear's Macaw) is one of the rarest. Once it was thought to be extinct, known only from a few stuffed specimens kept in museums. Then a small number were found living along a dry river-bed in Brazil. It happened that they were living within a protected nature reserve, but this has not made it any safer for the Indigo Macaw. Bird collectors and egg thieves are now a major threat to its survival.

24 One of the most endangered of all animals in South America is the **Golden Lion Marmoset**, so-called because of its lion-like bushy mane. There are very, very few of these striking primates alive in the forests of Brazil – its last stronghold. There are two main reasons why it is in danger of dying out. As with many other threatened animals in South America, the destruction of the forests is one very obvious reason. But there is another, more sinister reason. A creature as beautiful as the Golden Lion Marmoset is in danger from being caught alive and sold to animal collectors – anywhere in the world. This is strictly illegal but the practice still goes on in secret. The Golden Lion Marmoset has been bred in captivity and some have been put back into the wild.

North and East Africa and the Middle East

Algeria, Bahrain, Cyprus, Djibouti, Egypt, Ethiopia, Iran, Iraq, Israel, Jordan, Kuwait, Lebanon, Libya, Mauritania, Morocco, Oman, Qatar, Republic of Yemen, Saudi Arabia, Somali Republic, Sudan, Syria, Tunisia, Turkey, United Arab Emirates, Western Sahara

25 An endangered bird of North Africa and the Middle East is the **Northern Bald Ibis**. It was known to the Ancient Egyptians who included it in their heiroglyphic writing. But today there are none living in Egypt. The main colony is in Turkey and smaller ones are thousands of miles to the west in Algeria and Morocco. In Turkey, the Northern Bald Ibis has declined due to pesticides being used on the grasslands and marshes where it lives. However, natural causes, not man-made ones, may also be to blame. Its eggs are round and roll out of the nest and break. Its young fall out too.

26 The **Leopard** has been ruthlessly hunted for its valuable, spotted fur. It is almost extinct over most of its former range in North Africa and the Middle East, though small groups survive in isolated places. It is a protected animal in all of the countries where it exists, but even though parks and reserves have been established, poachers still find it and kill it. Fortunately, the Leopard has bred well in zoos. Even if it does die out in the wild, there will still be some alive in captivity.

27 The **Walia Ibex** lives in the highlands of Ethiopia, especially the Simien Mountains which have been declared a national park. If this area had not been protected as a park, then the Walia Ibex may have died out by now. But despite this attempt at saving it, hunters still enter the park and kill the Walia Ibex – so its future is by no means clear. It is one of Africa's rarest mammals.

28 In the Horn of Africa, the peninsula area in which the countries of Ethiopia and the Somali Republic are situated, lives **Grevy's Zebra**, the largest of all zebras. The herds in which it lives have grown smaller since the 1970s, and now it is known to be an endangered animal. The main threat to this small horse is from illegal hunting by poachers who kill it for its skin.

29 The **White-Tailed Fish-Eagle** is declining in many parts of the world, and in the Middle East its population is now very small. Pollution of the fish it eats is the danger to its survival. Protecting the White-Tailed Fish-Eagle is difficult. It will travel long distances in search of food with the risk that it will eat poisoned fish or bring it back to its young.

30 Extinction nearly happened to the **Arabian Oryx** in the 1970s. Once it was found throughout the countries of the Middle East, where it was plentiful. By the 1960s its population had fallen and it was found only in some of the wealthy oil-producing countries. This is when its final plight began. It became a popular 'sport' to hunt the Arabian Oryx, shooting at it from aeroplanes, helicopters and desert jeeps. The hunting was on an organized scale. In 1972 the last herd of seven Arabian Oryx living in the wild (in Oman) was killed. Fortunately, some had already been rescued and taken to a zoo in Arizona, in the United States. The climate there was similar to that of the Middle East, and the Arabian Oryx survived and bred successfully. In 1980 a few were taken back to Oman and set free in the wild, while others are now living in special reserves in Jordan.

Common name	25 Northern Bald Ibis	26 Leopard	27 Walia Ibex	28 Grevy's Zebra	29 White-Tailed Fish-Eagle	30 Arabian Oryx
Scientific name	Geronticus eremita	Panthera pardus	Capra walie	Equus grevyi	Haliaeetus albicilla	Oryx leucoryx
Where found	Algeria, Morocco, Turkey	Algeria, Israel, Morocco, Tunisia	Ethiopia	Ethiopia, Somali Republic	Iran, Iraq, Turkey	Jordan, Oman
Main dangers	Pesticides, hunting, natural causes	Hunting	Hunting, loss of habitat	Hunting	Pollution	Hunting
How rare?	***	****	*****	**	**	****

Central, West and South Africa

Angola, Benin, Botswana, Burkina Faso, Burundi, Cameroon, Central African Republic, Chad, Congo, Equatorial Guinea, Gabon, Gambia, Ghana, Guinea, Guinea-Bissau, Ivory Coast, Kenya, Lesotho, Liberia, Madagascar, Malawi, Mali, Mozambique, Namibia, Niger, Nigeria, Rwanda, Senegal, Sierra Leone, South Africa, Swaziland, Tanzania, Togo, Uganda, Zambia, Zaire, Zimbabwe

33 Scavenging on the bodies of dead cattle in South Africa is the **Cape Vulture**. In the past, meat-eating animals (such as lions) would feed off a dead creature first. They would crunch up the animal's bones and small pieces would later be eaten by the vulture and fed to its young. The calcium in the bones helped the young vultures to grow strong. But today there are fewer meat-eaters in South Africa and the Cape Vulture has not been able to get enough calcium. To protect this bird, special feeding stations have been made. At these 'vulture restaurants' the Cape Vulture eats from carcasses where the bones have been deliberately smashed.

31 Organized and illegal hunting by poachers has brought the **White Rhinoceros** close to extinction. Throughout Africa, armed gangs in fast trucks have killed thousands for their horns. The White Rhinoceros has two horns and, unfortunately, they are wanted by people from other countries, where they are made into knife handles or ground into so-called medicine powder. In order to save it, wildlife rangers have caught some and carefully removed their horns. Then the animals are released – minus their horns and unattractive to poachers.

32 There is only one penguin native to Africa – the **Jackass Penguin**. It lives off the coast of Namibia and South Africa where it is in danger from oil pollution, starvation, (caused by fishermen taking too many pilchards), and persecution. Too many of its eggs have been taken for food, and the result is that it has begun to die out. The Jackass Penguin was once one of Africa's most abundant sea-birds. Now it has become an endangered species – a fate which too many of the continent's animals have suffered.

Common name	31 White Rhinoceros	32 Jackass Penguin	33 Cape Vulture	34 African Elephant	35 Mountain Gorilla	36 Indris
Scientific name	Ceratotherium simum	Spheniscus demersus	Gyps coprotheres	Loxodonta africana	Gorilla gorilla beringei	Indri indri
Where found	South Africa, Zaire	Namibia, South Africa	South Africa	Kenya, Uganda, Central & West Africa	Rwanda, Uganda, Zaire	Madagascar
Main dangers	Hunting	Pollution, disturbance, persecution	Pesticides, disturbance	Hunting	Hunting, loss of habitat	Loss of habitat
How rare?	****	**	**	***	****	***

34 The plight of the **African Elephant** is well known. It is the largest living land animal – but for how much longer? Poachers have killed it by the thousand and attempts to protect it have not been very successful. The poachers kill the African Elephant for its ivory tusks which are illegally exported to countries where they can be carved into ornaments. Once, the African Elephant was a common sight across much of Africa. Today, its herds are smaller than before and it is found in far fewer countries.

35 Within the large area covered by Rwanda, Uganda and Zaire, the **Mountain Gorilla** is confined to a small patch of rainforest on the borders of all three countries. Here it is in danger as local people cut the rainforest down to make way for farming land. Their cattle graze in the forest, taking food from the Mountain Gorilla. It is a protected animal, living in national parks. But despite this, hunters still make their way to its remote home.

36 The **Indris** lives in rainforests on the island of Madagascar. In the past it was protected by the taboos of local people. They saw the Indris as one of their ancestors and would never cause it harm. But now the rainforest is being cut down and the Indris is losing its home. The demands to turn the forest into land for agriculture are great. To save the Indris, parts of the forest are now reserves where it can live safely.

Asia – China, Japan and the USSR

China, Hong Kong, Japan, Macao, Mongolia, North Korea, South Korea, Taiwan, Xizang (Tibet), Union of Soviet Socialist Republics (USSR: east of the Urals)

Common name	37 Giant Panda	38 Siberian Tiger	39 Wild Camel	40 Giant Salamander	41 Mandarin Duck	42 Père David's Deer
Scientific name	Ailuropoda melanoleuca	Panthera tigris altaica	Camelus bactrianus	Andrias japonicus	Aix galericulata	Elaphurus davidianus
Where found	China	Siberia (USSR)	China, Mongolia	Japan	China, Japan, North Korea, South Korea	China
Main dangers	Natural causes, hunting	Hunting, loss of habitat	Hunting, persecution	Hunting, loss of habitat	Loss of habitat	Hunting
How rare?	*****	*****	****	***	**	****

(37)

(39)

37 The bamboo forests of China are home to the **Giant Panda** – probably the world's best known endangered animal. It has never been a very common animal and it seems that its population has been falling quite naturally for hundreds of years. It is a protected animal and is respected by the people who live near it. However, poachers have sometimes killed the Giant Panda for its thick, woolly fur. Natural events are the main threat to its survival. Bamboo thickets may die, leaving the Giant Panda with little to eat.

38 Hunting and loss of natural habitat are the main dangers for the **Siberian Tiger**. It is the largest of all the tigers and one of the rarest. Hunters have tracked it down in its snowy Siberian homeland, attracted by its striped fur. There are very few left in the wild, and it is unlikely that any live outside of the special nature reserves which have been built to look after the Siberian Tiger.

39 In the remote deserts of China and Mongolia lives the **Wild Camel**. It is a familiar animal because there are many of them living in zoos around the world. But there are not very many left in the wild. Hunting for meat by local people is the main danger to the Wild Camel. Now it is a carefully protected animal and those that survive in the wild live in nature reserves. It is also called the Bactrian Camel.

40 No one knows how rare the **Giant Salamander** really is. It comes from Japan where it lives in fast-flowing mountain streams. At nearly two metres long, it is the world's largest amphibian. It is hunted in Japan, despite this practice being banned since the 1950s. The Giant Salamander is eaten as a delicacy and parts of its body are used in medicines. Another danger is caused by the blocking of streams where the Giant Salamander lives which destroys its natural habitat.

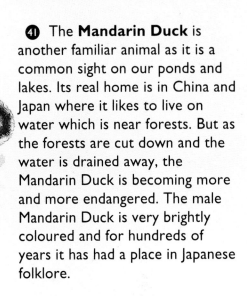

41 The **Mandarin Duck** is another familiar animal as it is a common sight on our ponds and lakes. Its real home is in China and Japan where it likes to live on water which is near forests. But as the forests are cut down and the water is drained away, the Mandarin Duck is becoming more and more endangered. The male Mandarin Duck is very brightly coloured and for hundreds of years it has had a place in Japanese folklore.

42 **Père David's Deer** is an animal that has been saved from certain extinction. This species of deer was not known outside China before the 1860s. They were made known to people in Europe by a French missionary who discovered them living in a park in China. Some were sent to countries in Europe to be studied, and this is how Père David's Deer came to be saved. Not long after, a great flood in China drowned many of the deer that lived in the park. Those which survived were killed for food by the starving population of Peking. The deer in Europe had young, and gradually a large herd was established at Woburn Abbey, England. In the 1980s some Père David's Deer were returned to China, so that a new herd could be started.

Asia – India and the Far East

Afghanistan, Bangladesh, Bhutan, Burma, Cambodia, India, Indonesia, Laos, Malaya, Nepal, Pakistan, The Philippines, Singapore, Sri Lanka, Thailand, Vietnam

(43)

44 On the Indonesian islands of Borneo and Sumatra lives the **Orang-utan**. This large, shy ape, has been hunted for its meat by local people for hundreds of years. Until the practice was stopped it was also hunted for zoo collections, and this involved killing a mother Orang-utan in order to take her young. Forest clearance is the main danger to the Orang-utan. The hardwood trees of its forest home are being felled by the timber trade.

(45)

43 Afghanistan and India are home to the **Snow Leopard**, where it lives among snow-covered mountains. It has very thick, spotted fur which protects it from the cold. In the countries where it lives it is protected by law, but this has not stopped hunters from killing it for its fur which they sell in local markets. The Snow Leopard hunts for deer which are being forced higher into the mountains by farmers' sheep invading their territory. If the Snow Leopard kills a sheep, then farmers set traps for it.

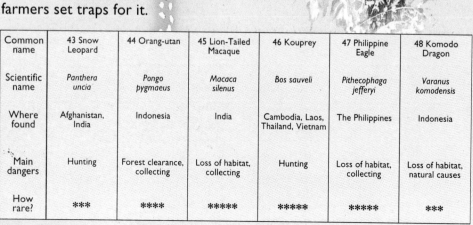

(44)

45 Increased farming in India has led directly to the decline of the **Lion-Tailed Macaque**. This small, black and white monkey lives in the country's tropical forests and as the world's demand for tea and coffee has grown, the forests have been cleared to make way for plantations. While some animals have managed to adapt to new environments, the Lion-Tailed Macaque avoids the tea and coffee plantations completely. It has also been the victim of animal hunters who have taken young macaques for illegal export to collectors around the world. To capture a young Lion-Tailed Macaque the hunters have been quite prepared to kill its parents.

Common name	43 Snow Leopard	44 Orang-utan	45 Lion-Tailed Macaque	46 Kouprey	47 Philippine Eagle	48 Komodo Dragon
Scientific name	Panthera uncia	Pongo pygmaeus	Macaca silenus	Bos sauveli	Pithecophaga jefferyi	Varanus komodensis
Where found	Afghanistan, India	Indonesia	India	Cambodia, Laos, Thailand, Vietnam	The Philippines	Indonesia
Main dangers	Hunting	Forest clearance, collecting	Loss of habitat, collecting	Hunting	Loss of habitat, collecting	Loss of habitat, natural causes
How rare?	***	****	*****	*****	*****	***

46 The **Kouprey** is a large wild ox which lives in south-east Asia. It is one of the world's largest mammals and is near extinction. Before 1937, the Kouprey was completely unknown to science. Since its discovery the countries where it is found have stopped hunting it. They have made plans to protect the Kouprey in special reserves where they hope it will breed.

47 The old name for the **Philippine Eagle** was the Monkey-eating Eagle. It is one of the world's most endangered eagles and lives on the small islands of The Philippines, where it soars above the tree-covered slopes of ancient volcanoes. A large bird of prey, it hunts for deer, birds, snakes and monkeys – which is how it got its old name. As the hardwood trees of its forest home are felled, the Philippine Eagle population is falling. Illegal trading by animal collectors is also to blame for its downfall.

48 Some small Indonesian islands are the home of the **Komodo Dragon** – the largest lizard in the world which grows to three metres long. It lives in forests and along sandy beaches, where it digs long burrows. Scientists have discovered that there are more males than females alive and they think this is why the Komodo Dragon is slowly dying out. Also, the natural vegetation of the islands where it lives is changing, and the Komodo Dragon does not seem to be adapting very well to the new environment. For this animal, natural causes may one day result in its extinction.

Australasia

Australia, Papua New Guinea, New Zealand, Melanesia, Micronesia, Polynesia

49 In a country as large as Australia it is possible for an animal to disappear without trace for years. One such animal is **Leadbeater's Possum** which was first discovered in the middle of the last century – but it was not until the middle of this century that it was seen again. Scientists had thought that it was extinct. Leadbeater's Possum lives in the Mountain Ash forests of south-east Australia, where its main threat is from tree felling. It is also in danger from fires which can easily burn all the leaves off the Mountain Ash trees.

49

50

Common name	49 Leadbeater's Possum	50 Bridled Nail-Tailed Wallaby	51 Kakapo	52 Numbat	53 Takahe	54 Tuatara
Scientific name	*Gymnobelideus leadbeateri*	*Onychogalea fraenata*	*Strigops habroptilus*	*Myrmecobius fasciatus*	*Notornis mantelli*	*Sphenodon punctatus*
Where found	Australia	Australia	New Zealand	Australia	New Zealand	New Zealand
Main dangers	Loss of habitat, fires	Loss of habitat, predators	Loss of habitat, predators	Loss of habitat, predators, fires	Loss of habitat, predators, hunting, natural causes	Domesticated animals
How rare?	*****	*****	****	****	****	***

50 The **Bridled Nail-Tailed Wallaby** of east Australia gets its name from the white stripes on its shoulders which have a similar shape to a horse's bridle. Not that long ago it was one of Australia's most common wallabys, but now it is one of the rarest. Its decline is due to three main reasons. The forests and plains where the Bridled Nail-Tailed Wallaby used to live have been turned into grazing land for sheep and cattle. Also, foxes (introduced by man) have attacked it while rabbits have taken its food.

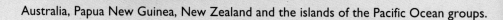
Australia, Papua New Guinea, New Zealand and the islands of the Pacific Ocean groups.

52 The **Numbat** (also called the Banded Anteater) is found in open grassland and woodland. It lives off a diet of insects and larvae and its long tongue can easily reach into a hollow log to search for termites. Predatory animals introduced into Australia by man, such as foxes, cats and dogs, have caused the decline of the once-common Numbat. It is also threatened by its habitat being cleared for agriculture and mining, and by grass fires.

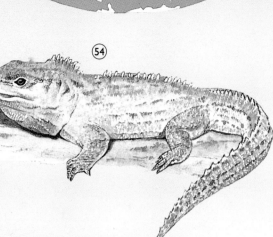

54 The **Tuatara** is a link with the past. In fact, most of its closest relatives died out millions of years ago with the dinosaurs. This 'living fossil' is found only on some small, uninhabited islands off the coast of New Zealand, where specially protected sanctuaries have been made for it. Without these places of safety, the Tuatara would find it difficult to survive. New Zealand's huge population of sheep would be to blame, eating the plants on which insects live – the food of the Tuatara.

51 In New Zealand are several birds which have lost the power of flight. This is because they have no natural enemies – so there is no need to fly to safety. But for the **Kakapo**, an owl-like parrot which lives on South Island, the arrival of European settlers over the last two centuries has signalled danger. Their rats, cats and dogs have found the defenceless Kakapo easy prey. Now it occurs only in very small numbers. It faces a difficult future as it is almost impossible to protect it from the modern predators.

53 The **Takahe** also lives in New Zealand. It too is a flightless bird in constant danger from attacks by predators. Once it was thought to be extinct, but in the 1940s a few were rediscovered living in the thick undergrowth and forests on South Island. Apart from rats and other new predators, the Takahe has been hunted for hundreds of years by the New Zealand Maori people for food. Probably the main cause of its decline has been the loss of its forest home, caused by gradual changes in New Zealand's climate – a natural danger, not a man-made one.

Oceans and Seas

Oceans – Arctic, Atlantic, Indian, Pacific, Southern
Principal Seas – Adriatic, Aegean, Arabian, Baltic, Barents, Bering, Black, Caribbean, Caspian, Mediterranean, North, Red, Tyrrhenian

55 There are few whales which have not been hunted to the verge of extinction. The **Bowhead Whale** (also known as the Greenland Right Whale, because it was once the 'right' whale to hunt) has been killed for its oil and whalebone. It has been a protected animal for many years now, but as its population has fallen so low, it has still not risen to the point at which its survival is ensured.

56 For the animals that live in the seas and oceans of the world, hunting is the main danger they face. The **Hooded Seal** lives in cold northern waters stretching from Canada and Greenland in the west to Iceland and Norway in the east. The male is very distinctive because it has a pouch, or hood, of pink skin above its nose which it inflates when it becomes excited. Over-hunting has seriously affected the population of the Hooded Seal. Both the young and adults are killed. The young are taken for their skins and adults for their meat, fat and oil.

57 A similar fate has befallen Europe's most endangered mammal – the **Mediterranean Monk Seal**. For centuries it has been hunted by fishermen in the Mediterranean Sea who have blamed it for stealing their fish and damaging their nets. Today it is strictly protected, but now there are new dangers to its survival. Tourism has affected the beaches where it used to come ashore and the badly polluted water of the Mediterranean has harmed its chances of living. The survival of the Mediterranean Monk Seal depends on the success of special reserves in Greece and Turkey.

58 The same is true for the **Blue Whale** – the largest animal alive today. But for how much longer will it be with us? Excessive hunting in all the world's oceans has reduced its numbers to a level from which it may never recover, despite it now being listed as a protected animal. Oil, meat and bone are why the Blue Whale has been killed. Alternatives to each of these products could have been found, but now it may be too late to save the Blue Whale from extinction. Unlike a land animal, it cannot be placed in a special reserve. For those that still live in the oceans they must hope the hunters never return.

(59)

Common name	55 Bowhead Whale	56 Hooded Seal	57 Mediterranean Monk Seal	58 Blue Whale	59 Narwhal	60 Loggerhead Turtle
Scientific name	*Balaena mysticetus*	*Cystophora cristata*	*Monachus monachus*	*Balaenoptera musculus*	*Monodon monoceros*	*Caretta caretta*
Where found	Arctic Ocean, North Atlantic Ocean	Arctic Ocean, North Atlantic Ocean	Aegean Sea, Mediterranean Sea	All oceans	Arctic Ocean	Atlantic Ocean, Black Sea, Mediterranean Sea
Main dangers	Hunting, population not sustainable	Hunting	Hunting, pollution, persecution	Hunting, population not sustainable	Hunting	Hunting, pollution, loss of habitat, netting
How rare?	*****	***	*****	*****	***	****

59 The **Narwhal** is an incredible animal. Fishermen in the Middle Ages were attracted by the long, spiralled tusk of the male, and they would tell tales of how they had caught a Unicorn. The tusk is actually its extended left tooth. It lives in the Arctic Ocean, close to the North Pole and amongst the pack-ice of the cold sea. The danger to the Narwhal is from hunting by the Eskimos of Canada and Greenland.

60 Another of the Mediterranean's threatened species is the **Loggerhead Turtle**. Hunting for its meat and shell have been the main dangers in the past. But now it has to contend with the loss of the sandy beaches where it lays its eggs. New hotels have been built on its breeding sites in Turkey. The hotels are for tourists, and when they arrive in the area they too add to the disturbance of the Loggerhead Turtle. Even out at sea it is not safe, since it can become entangled in fishing nets and drown.

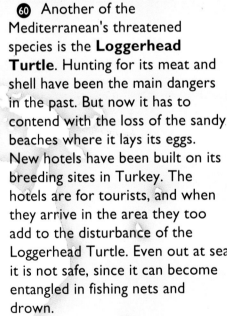
(60)

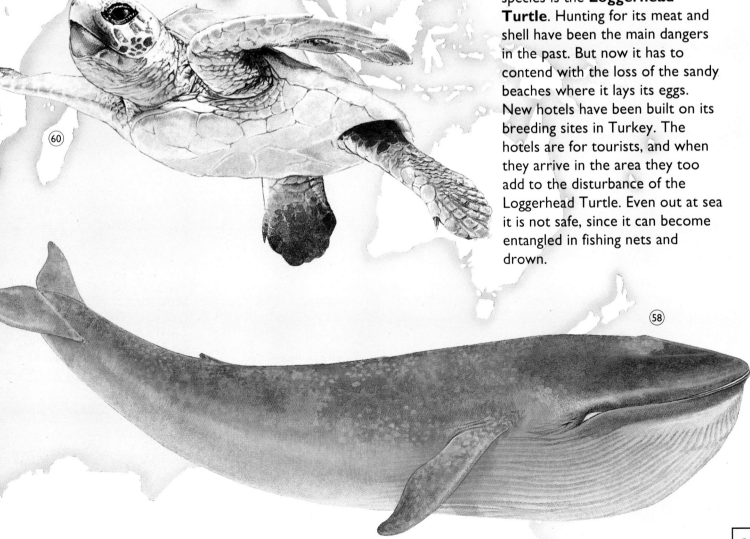
(58)

How endangered animals can be saved

What is being done to save endangered animals? All over the world people are working to save animals from extinction. There are organizations such as the Fauna and Flora Preservation Society (FFPS), Greenpeace, the International Union for Conservation of Nature and Natural Resources (IUCN), and the World Wide Fund for Nature (WWF). Each organization mounts special campaigns to make people more aware of the plight of the world's animals.

Here are seven ways in which endangered animals can be saved:

1 Habitat protection The places where animals live in the wild need to be preserved. Some animals are found in just one place – destroying it might mean destroying that animal too.

2 International agreements
Decisions made between different countries can protect animals. For instance, many countries have now agreed to stop hunting the Blue Whale – but not all countries have joined in, so the protection is not complete.

3 Captive breeding Some very rare animals have been bred in captivity and the species has been saved – the Arabian Oryx is a good example.

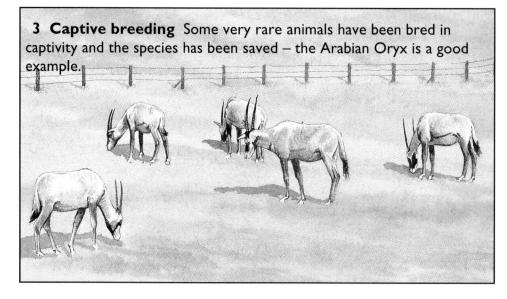

4 Parks and reserves Where endangered animals are alive in the wild, the places where they live have been made into parks or reserves. In these places it is forbidden to harm the animals or destroy their habitat.

5 Alternative products

Many animals – such as whales – are killed to provide goods for man. But often these products can come from other sources which do not injure animals. Artificial fur and vegetable oils are better than killing rare animals for the fur and oil which they can provide.

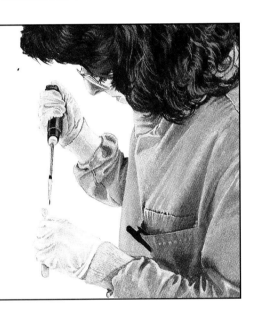

6 Gene banks

Scientists are experimenting with this new technique which may or may not prove useful. They are keeping in suspended animation an animal's genetic material (the 'building blocks' of life) from which it might be possible in the future to 'grow' a new animal of the same kind.

KEYWORDS

Common name The ordinary name for an animal.

Endangered This is when an animal is in danger of dying out.

Extinct This is when all the animals of one kind have died out.

Food chain The link between living things whereby energy is transferred by one thing eating another.

Habitat The natural place for an animal to live.

Pesticide Chemicals which are used to control harmful pests.

Polluted When the place where an animal lives becomes dirty, then that place has become polluted.

Protected animal An animal which it has been agreed not to hurt.

Reserve A special place where an animal can live in safety.

Scientific name The Latin name which experts give an animal.

7 Education

This is probably the easiest, the cheapest and the best way of saving animals – whether they are endangered or not. The more we know about animals, such as where and how they live, then we will be better equipped to care for them.

Education is also about understanding our own mistakes. It is wrong to cut down too much of the world's rainforests or take too many fish from the seas, as we are only just beginning to learn. The future for the animals of our world depends on keeping 'sustainable populations' alive – populations where the numbers are big enough for the animals to survive on their own. For the 500 animals which are already extinct because of man, their populations fell below a sustainable level. Mistakes were made with animals such as the Dodo, the Great Auk and the Quagga, and now they have vanished from the face of the Earth for ever. As for the 4,500 animals today listed as endangered, some will almost certainly become extinct. But for others there will be a happy ending, and whether by good fortune, their own or man's doing, they will survive.

Arctic

Scandin

North
Europe

South Eur

North
Africa

North
America

West
Africa

Atlantic
Ocean

Central
America

Pacific
Ocean

South
America

Atlantic
Ocean